Date: February 21, 2008

To: Dotty

From: Margaret

Enjoy!

Laura Ingalls Wilder's
Prairie
Wisdom

Laura Ingalls Wilder's
Prairie Wisdom

YVONNE POPE

**Andrews McMeel
Publishing**

Kansas City

06 07 08 09 10 TWP 10 9 8 7 6 5 4 3 2 1

ISBN-13: 978-0-7407-5721-1
ISBN-10: 0-7407-5721-0

Library of Congress Control Number: 2005932781

www.andrewsmcmeel.com

Quotes have been preserved as faithfully as possible; however, grammar, punctuation, and spelling have been updated to modern standards.

ATTENTION: SCHOOLS AND BUSINESSES

Andrews McMeel books are available at quantity discounts with bulk purchase for educational, business, or sales promotional use. For information, please write to: Special Sales Department, Andrews McMeel Publishing, LLC, 4520 Main Street, Kansas City, Missouri 64111.

THIS BOOK IS DEDICATED
TO MY LOVING FAMILY.

Thank you, Randy, Joseph, and Rachel,
for your love and constant support.

ACKNOWLEDGMENTS

Grateful acknowledgement is given to the following organizations and individuals:

First to God, for the artistic ability.

Stephen W. Hines, editor of *Little House in the Ozarks: The Rediscovered Writings.* This book was my inspiration.

Farm Progress Companies, for articles used by permission.

Laura Crane, for her research assistance.

Reverend Bob Roark, for continual encouragement.

The State Historical Society of Missouri, for the release of microfilm.

Editor Katie Anderson, for her guidance.

INTRODUCTION

*A*pproximately twenty years prior to writing the popular Little House series, Laura Ingalls Wilder wrote for a Mansfield, Missouri, regional newspaper. Her articles and essays centered on farming, world events, and home-oriented values. Laura's homespun wisdom and amusing personality shine in these quotes taken from her writings; her wisdom transcends the years.

The true way to live is to enjoy every moment as it passes, and surely it is in the everyday things around us that the beauty of life lies.

I ran away from a thousand things
waiting to be done and stole a little
visit with a friend.

We who live in quiet places have the opportunity to become acquainted with ourselves, to think our own thoughts.

*I*f we have less sympathy and understanding for others and are more selfish than we used to be, it is time to take a new path.

Things and persons appear to the light we throw upon them.

Let us be careful that our homes
are furnished with pleasant and
happy thoughts.

Our hearts are mostly in the right place, but we seem to be weak in the head.

However fleeting and changeable life may appear to be on the surface, we know that the great underlying values of life are always the same.

*T*here is no turning back nor
standing still; we must go forward,
into the future, generation after generation, toward the accomplishment of
the ends that have been set for the
human race.

There are pleasant things to think about and beauty to be found everywhere, and they grow by dwelling on them.

No one ever achieved anything
from the smallest object to the greatest
unless the dream was dreamed first.

It is not to our efforts alone that our measure of success is due, but to the life principle in the earth and the seed, to the sunshine and the rain—to the goodness of God.

Perhaps it is our spirit and attitude toward life and its conditions that are giving us trouble, instead of a shortage of time.

The kingdom of home, as well as the kingdom of heaven, is within us.

*T*here is no standing still. The moment that growth stops, decay sets in.

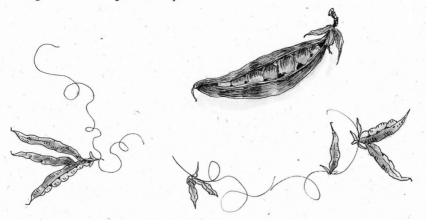

Wake up to your opportunities.

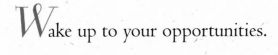

Let's be cheerful! We have no more right to steal the brightness out of the day for our own family than we have to steal the purse of a stranger.

I am sure we all know in our hearts we have a great deal for which to be thankful. In spite of disappointment and weariness and sorrow, His goodness and mercy does follow us all the days of our lives.

*M*ore than material blessings, let us, with humble hearts, give thanks for the revelation to us and our better understanding of the greatness and goodness of God.

I am a child again and a longing unutterable fills my heart for mother's counsel.

*A*s the years pass, I am coming more and more to understand that it is the common everyday blessings of our common everyday lives for which we should be particularly grateful.

Make your little
farm home noted for its
hospitality and the social
times you have there.

Mankind is not following a blind trail; feet were set upon the true path in the beginning.

Life is a good collector, and sooner or later the account must be paid in full.

We may be friendly and courteous and still hold frankly to our honest convictions.

I have concluded that whether it is sad to grow old depends on how we face it, whether we are looking forward with confidence or backward with regret.

Are we coming to a cheerful old age, or are we being beaten and cowed by the years as they pass?

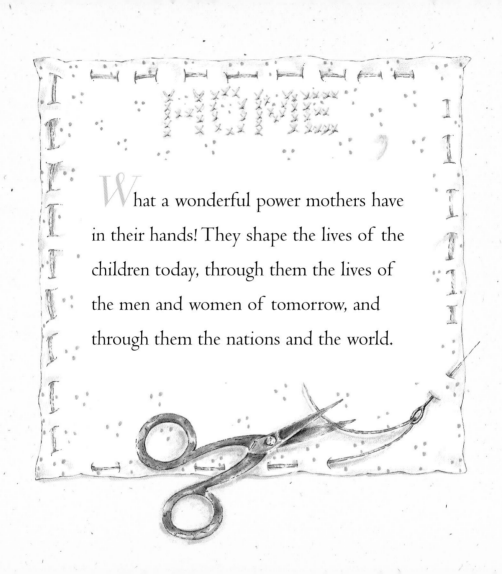

HOME,

What a wonderful power mothers have in their hands! They shape the lives of the children today, through them the lives of the men and women of tomorrow, and through them the nations and the world.

We can teach this love of home to the children and it will help to hold them steady when their time comes.

*It seems to be a law of nature
that everything and every person
must move along.*

*I*f popular favor must be paid for by surrender of principles or loss in character, then indeed the price is too high.

*T*he sweetness of life lies in usefulness, like honey deep in the heart of clover bloom.

There is no time like the early morning, when the
spirit of light broods over the earth at its awakening.

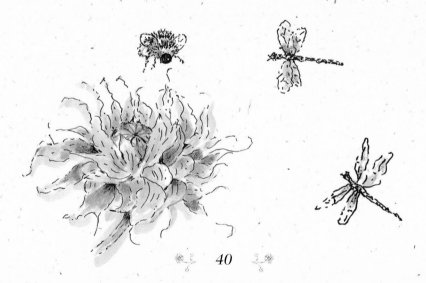

The colors in the sky at sunset, the delicate tints
of the early spring foliage, the brilliant autumn
leaves, the softly colored grasses and lovely flowers—
what painter ever equaled their beauties with paint
and brush?

One of the greatest safeguards against becoming old is to keep growing mentally.

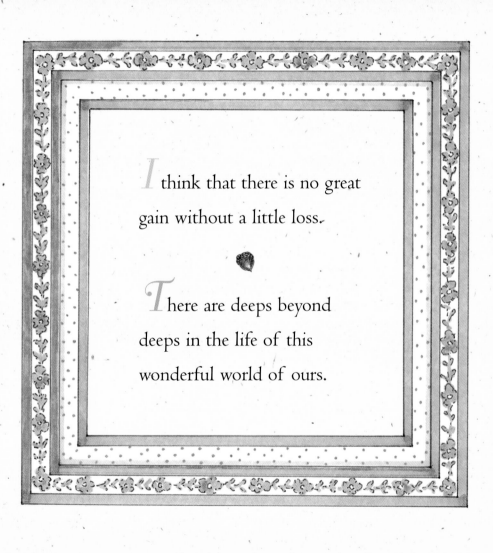

I think that there is no great
gain without a little loss.

*T*here are deeps beyond
deeps in the life of this
wonderful world of ours.

This little farm home is a delightful place for friends to come for afternoon tea under the trees.

A bird's song will set the steps to music all day long.

*H*ave you seen any fairies lately, or have you allowed the harder facts of life to dull your "seeing eye"?

Thanksgiving will soon be here and it is time to be getting our blessings in order.

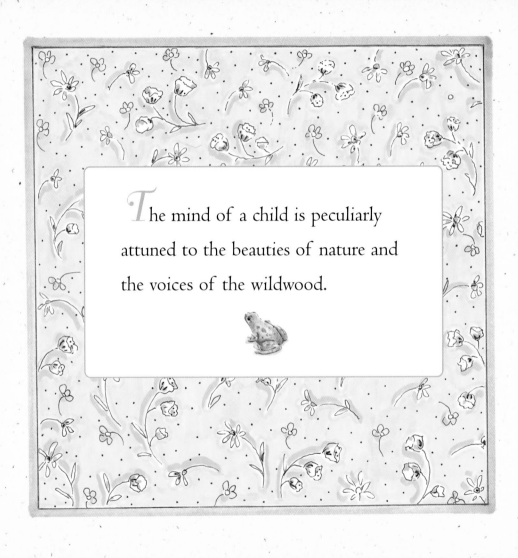

*T*he mind of a child is peculiarly
attuned to the beauties of nature and
the voices of the wildwood.

Fairies still appear to those with seeing eyes.

I have a feeling that childhood has been robbed of a great deal of its joys by taking away its belief in wonderful, mystic things, in fairies and all their kin.

*T*he world is the beautiful estate of the human family passing down from generation to generation.

Sometimes we are inclined to wish our childhood days might come again.

As far back as I can remember the old times were good times.

*I*f we make good neighbors of ourselves,
we likely shall not need to seek new friends
in strange places.

We inherit the earth,
the great round world that
is God's footstool.

Out in the meadow, I picked a wild sunflower, and as I looked into its golden heart such a wave of homesickness came over me.

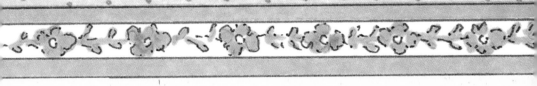

We are the heirs of the ages.

A moment's pause to watch the glory of a sunset is soul satisfying.

We should be willing to allow others the freedom we demand for ourselves.

*I*t seems such a pity that
we can learn to value what
we have only through the
loss of it.

*H*ow much pleasanter it would be and how much more would be accomplished if we did not give our word unless we intended to keep it, so that we would all know what we could depend upon.

One's word is of infinitely
more worth than money.

*H*ave you seen any fairies lately? I asked the question of a little girl not long ago. "Huh! There's no such thing as fairies," she replied. In some way the answer hurt me, and I have been vaguely disquieted when I have thought of it ever since. By the way, have you seen any fairies lately? Please do not answer as the little girl did, for I'm sure there are fairies and that you at least have seen their work.

*N*othing is ever gained by
allowing anger to have sway.

*A*nger is a destroying force. What all the world needs is its opposite—an uplifting power.

There is a great satisfaction

in a task accomplished.

*T*he old way was best, for it takes about six days of work to give just the right flavor to a day off.

*I*t belittles us to think of our daily tasks as small things, and if we continue to do so, it will in time make us small.

We are so overwhelmed with things these days that our lives are all, more or less, cluttered.

Such magic there is in Christmas to draw
the absent ones home and if unable to go in the
body, the thoughts will hover there! Our hearts
grow tender with childhood memories and love
of kindred, and we are better throughout the
year for having, in spirit, become a child again
at Christmastime.

*T*he safest course is to be as understanding as possible, and where our understanding fails call charity to its aid.

*M*emories! We go through life collecting them.

*The voices of nature do
not speak so plainly to us as
we grow older.*

*Y*outh ever gazes forward while age is inclined to look back.

*T*hough old age has gray hair and twinges of rheumatism, remember that childhood has freckles, tonsils, and the measles.

$\mathcal{A}$ good laugh overcomes more difficulties and dissipates more dark clouds than any other one thing.

*T*o laugh and forget is one of the saving graces.

As the New Year comes, seemingly with ever-increasing swiftness, there is a feeling that life is too short to accomplish the things we must do.

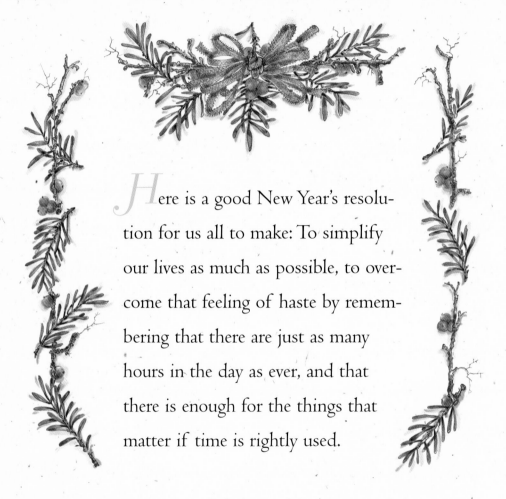

*H*ere is a good New Year's resolution for us all to make: To simplify our lives as much as possible, to overcome that feeling of haste by remembering that there are just as many hours in the day as ever, and that there is enough for the things that matter if time is rightly used.

*T*he future is in our hands
to make it what we will.